(66 2)

PRAYERS

FOR ALL OCCASIONS

Prayers

FOR

All Occasions

A Book of Short Prayers
for Everyday Life
by
STUART R. OGLESBY

JOHN KNOX PRESS
Richmond, Virginia

NOTE.—*Quotations in this volume from the American
Standard Version are copyrighted, 1929, by the International Council of Religious Education, and used by per-
mission.*

DEDICATION

To the members of Central Presbyterian Church, Atlanta, Georgia,
who have used these prayers and
have been the inspiration of them,
this little book of worship is
gratefully dedicated.

MOST OF THE prayers that this book contains have been printed in the *Central Presbyterian Weekly*, Atlanta, Georgia. When the author, who is the present pastor of this church, began nine years ago the writing and publication of short prayers each week, he was surprised at the instant and cordial reception they received. Frequently during the years he has found these prayers clipped from the *Weekly* and being carried by members for daily use. Some have made scrapbooks in which they have pasted an accumulation of the prayers for many years.

Outside the membership of this church, those to whom our *Weekly* goes have given the prayers sympathetic reception, at times reproducing them for wider use.

These things have encouraged the author to believe that the simple and short prayers might have a still wider use in the church at large.

Humbly and gratefully this book is sent forth, with the hope that the God to whom we pray may cause it to be of service to many who feel the need of help from books of devotion and worship.

S. R. O.

THIS DEVOTIONAL BOOK, containing a variety of printed prayers, was written by the genial pastor of the Central Presbyterian Church, Atlanta, Georgia. Through nearly ten years of his ministry at Central the author has given especial attention to pastoral work, and thus has come to know intimately the needs, aspirations, and hopes of his people. This collection of brief meditations was developed through the years for use in the weekly church bulletin, and as such reflects a pastor's understanding of and devotion to and aspirations for a great congregation.

The style is clear, dignified, and forceful, lacking timeworn platitudes that for so many have become meaningless. The content is vital, reflecting those universal yearnings of the human heart felt by men and women in every walk of life. The note of earnestness, sincerity, and humility is apparent on every page. Man's desperate need, the sonship of Jesus, and the sovereignty of God are assumed throughout. Though recognizing the chaos and confusion existent in international and individual relationships, the element of despair is appropriately absent, and in its place is a clear confession of faith and confidence in the goodness of God.

I heartily commend this devotional volume to men and women who experience difficulty in giving expression to the deeper emotions of life, to ministers and others who seek greater effectiveness in public prayer, and to all who are helped by quiet, directed meditation.

PATRICK H. CARMICHAEL.

CONTENTS

INVOCATION

NOW THANK WE ALL OUR GOD

"Now thank we all our God
 With hearts and hands and voices,
Who wondrous things hath done,
 In whom His world rejoices;
Who, from our mothers' arms,
 Hath blessed us on our way
With countless gifts of love,
 And still is ours today."

PRAYERS

FOR EVERYDAY

SURPRISES

*"Unto him that is able to do exceeding
abundantly above all that we ask or
think."*—EPHESIANS 3:20.

OUR HEAVENLY FATHER, amidst
all the surprises of life, we pray that
Thou wilt surprise us by the length
of Thy patience, the depth of Thy
sympathy, and the breadth of Thy understanding. If we have thought that
Thou art altogether such a one as ourselves, reprove us this day and reveal
clearly to us that Thy thoughts are not
our thoughts nor Thy ways our ways.
As we kneel to pray, may Thy peace
which passeth understanding fill our
hearts; and as we go forth to serve, let
Thy heavenly joy shine from our faces.
Give us faith to believe that Thou canst
use us, with all our frailties, in Thy
Kingdom program, we ask in Jesus'
name. *Amen.*

CARRYING THROUGH

1

"Let us run with patience the race that is set before us."—HEBREWS 12:1.

O GOD, WE NEED Thy help that we may give ourselves in utmost sincerity to the completion of every task Thou dost lay upon us. Surely our burdens are not heavier than Thy grace is plentiful. Make us strong to do right and zealous in the pursuit of duty. Let us be joyful in sacrifice and consecrated in every portion of life. Suffer no good cause to languish because of our indifference, but may our earnest concern and active labor advance Thy Kingdom in all its phases and issues. In Jesus' name. *Amen.*

REFRESHMENT

1

*"Times of refreshing shall come from the
presence of the Lord."*—ACTS 3:19.

OUR FATHER, for the times of
refreshing that come from Thy presence, the Wells of Elim that we reach
in our travels through the desert sands
of trials and discouragement, we give
Thee thanks from the bottom of our
hearts. Surely no load is too heavy to
be borne, no duty too difficult to discharge, no task too hard to carry to
completion, when the Lord refreshes us
and renews our strength. Help us to
endure hardness as good soldiers of
Christ, and to rejoice if we are ever
counted worthy to suffer for Thy
name's sake. *Amen.*

LABORERS TOGETHER

1

*"I can do all things through Christ which
strengtheneth me."*—PHILIPPIANS 4:13.

O GOD, OUR FATHER, we beseech
Thee for wisdom and discernment as
we face the problems of our day, for
grace and strength as we take up our
tasks, and for courage and perseverance
as we discharge our duties. May we
have a vision of world needs, as well as
needs that are close at hand, and a confident assurance that Christ and His
gospel can meet every need. Use us, our
talents, our time, our possessions, in the
supplying of these needs, we pray. May
we help and encourage one another,
each day, in all the phases of Kingdom
work that Thy children are carrying
forward under the guidance of Thy
Holy Spirit. For Jesus' sake. *Amen.*

IN HIS STEPS

1

*"Follow that which is good, both among
yourselves, and to all men."*
—I THESSALONIANS 5:15.

OUR FATHER, let Thy presence
banish worry and fear from the hearts
of Thy children as we serve Thee day
by day. Help us to live upon such a
high plane of aspiration and endeavor
that the miasmic poisons of selfishness,
self-deception, and covetousness may
not enfeeble our characters nor bias our
minds. May we ever try to feel the emotions, think the thoughts, and perform
the deeds that are befitting to us as
Christians, whether this be easy, or
hard. This we ask for Jesus' sake.
Amen.

PEACE ON EARTH

1

"They that take the sword shall perish with the sword."—MATTHEW 26:52.

ALMIGHTY GOD, and Prince of Peace, teach us that it is not Thy will that men or nations should fight and kill and destroy. May Thy will become the will of Thy professed followers, and may all who are called by Thy name live at peace with God, with themselves, and with their fellow men. We pray that the advocates of peace may be stronger in their influence than the advocates of war, and that the principles of peace shall hold increasing sway over the peoples of the world. Hasten the time when wars shall cease unto the ends of the earth, we humbly pray in Jesus' name. *Amen.*

THE PRESENCE

1

"Lo, I am with you alway."
—MATTHEW 28:20.

OUR FATHER, make us more conscious in our daily lives of the presence of Jesus, who promised to be with us day by day unto the end. May we make every decision, perform every task, and face every experience as in His presence. Since sin and selfishness cause Him to disappear from our sight, so may we die unto sin and live unto righteousness through the strength that He imparts. Thus growing in grace, may we be given each day a clearer vision of His blessed face. In His name. *Amen.*

OUR CHURCH

1

"The church of the living God, the pillar and ground of the truth."—I TIMOTHY 3:15.

O GOD, WE THANK THEE for our Church, and for its many sacred ministries that we have enjoyed. Let us never grow indifferent to its work. May we ever be loyal to its program, efficient in the duties that are ours, and dependable in every assignment of service that is laid upon us. As members of the organization that represents Christ on earth and that fights His battles, we would be urgent in season and out of season in doing with our might the things our hands find to do. In His name we pray. *Amen.*

SEERS

1

*"He that is now called a Prophet was before-
time called a Seer."*—I SAMUEL 9:9.

OUR FATHER, for all the lovely
things of life we give Thee our grateful thanks. We rejoice in the cleansing
and purifying effect upon our souls
of great music, great paintings, great
scenery. May our eyes never be closed
to real beauty, nor our souls insensi-
tive to that which is pleasing, harmonious, and inspiring. We thank Thee,
God, for those who can see more deeply
and more clearly than we can and, at
the same time, interpret more discern-
ingly the wondrous things Thou hast
made. Open the eyes of us all that we
may behold the surpassing beauties of
Thy creation. In Jesus' name. *Amen.*

HEROISM

1

"He that loseth his life for my sake shall find it."—MATTHEW 10:39.

OUR FATHER IN HEAVEN, teach us to rejoice in the trials of life that shake us from our lethargy and ease and develop within us heroic traits of endurance and sacrifice. Help us to recognize Thee when Thou dost appear in the midst of the storm, as well as when Thou comest in the peaceful quietness of a summer's day. Cause all our experiences of Thee to strengthen within us the qualities of mind and heart that make us more like our Master. Grant that our attitudes in life, as well as our acts of service, may advance Thy cause and glorify Thy name. For Jesus' sake. *Amen.*

INVESTING LIFE

1

*"A vessel unto honour, sanctified, and meet for
the master's use."*—II TIMOTHY 2:21.

O GOD, with only one life to live,
it is the deep desire of our hearts to
invest that life in the very noblest and
best things. With so many demands we
are often bewildered as we make our
choices. Therefore, we look to Thee and
pray for Thy guidance and for Thy
wisdom. Help us, in the great house
that is Thy church, to be vessels unto
honor, sanctified and meet for the Master's use. By Thy grace, we would be
prepared unto every good work. In all
things let us glorify Thee, our Lord,
and thus make our lives count in Thy
service. In the Master's name. *Amen.*

RIGHT SHALL TRIUMPH

1

"The eyes of the Lord are upon the righteous."
—PSALM 34:15.

LORD, HELP US to believe uninterruptedly in the ultimate triumph of right and righteousness. At the same time, may we be convinced in our souls that no noble action, no courageous fight for truth and justice, and no sacrifice cheerfully sustained in the name of the Master and for the sake of His cause are ever without effect. Surely such things are not hidden from the eyes of the Judge of all the earth, who giveth His reward in due season. Therefore, make us always strong in the face of temptation, patient in suffering, loyal in duty, cheerful in spirit, and triumphant in life. We ask in Jesus' name. *Amen.*

STANDARDS OF WORTH

*"He that soweth to the Spirit shall . . . reap
life everlasting."*—GALATIANS 6:8.

OUR FATHER, may the fruit of the
Spirit show forth in our lives as we
seek to serve Thee. Keep us from the
error of confusing human standards
of accomplishment with the standards of spiritual growth as given in Thy
Word. Let us never sacrifice inward
realities for outward possessions. May
we be more concerned about the helpfulness of our lives and influence upon
others than about speaking words of
condemnation and rebuke. May we not
be overcome of evil, but always overcome evil with good. For Jesus' sake.
Amen.

MORE LIKE THE MASTER

1

"I am the way, the truth, and the life."
—JOHN 14:6.

Surely, O Lord, if our hearts were clean and our spirits right, we should have a better influence in this world of sorrow and suffering, of self-ishness and sin. Deliver us, therefore, we pray Thee, from self-deception, from self-righteousness, and from that type of self-assertiveness which alien-ates and repels. Make us, rather, so simple and so attractive in our religious lives, so bright and helpful in our human contacts, that men may be drawn by our example to the Saviour who is Himself the Way, the Truth, and the Life. In His name. *Amen.*

CHILDREN OF LIGHT

1

"Let your light so shine before men."
—MATTHEW 5:16.

OUR FATHER, release us from the inner forces of evil that so often overcome our will, color our thinking, and give loose rein to our emotions. May Christ in us be the Conqueror of evil in whatever form it attacks us, and thus become, not only the hope, but also the assurance of glory. May we, as children of light, continually let our light shine upon the darkness around us that men may see our good works and glorify our Father in heaven. For Jesus' sake. *Amen.*

THE GRACE OF REPENTANCE

"The goodness of God leadeth thee to repentance."—ROMANS 2:4.

OUR HEAVENLY FATHER, with deep humility, we confess our sins before Thee, both individual and national. We have too often forsaken the Fountain of Living Waters and hewn out for ourselves broken cisterns that can hold no water. We have let selfishness and sin obscure our vision of Thee and dull our sense of duty to our fellow men. Grant unto us the grace of repentance, of godly sorrow for sin. Turn us back from our willful strayings to the God of Bethel, by whose hand alone can come help and salvation. Quicken within us the sense of duty which has been dulled, and grant that God's goodness to us may make us alert to the needs of others. In Jesus' name. *Amen.*

HELPFULNESS

1

"Bear ye one another's burdens, and so fulfil the law of Christ."—GALATIANS 6:2.

OUR FATHER, we yearn for a better understanding of spiritual things and a closer walk with Thee that we may interpret aright the times in which we live. We long to be able to minister, according to Thy will and according to the example of Christ, to people who are troubled and burdened with the cares of the world. Instill into the hearts of Thy servants each day fresh confidence in Thy goodness. Deliver us from fear and worry that we may deal confidently with the fears and worries of others. Strengthen our faith and increase our capacity for sympathy and understanding. Make us glad to bear one another's burdens, and grateful for opportunities of fulfilling thus the law of Christ. In His name. *Amen.*

THE ISSUES OF THE DAY

1

"That we may do all the words of this law."
—DEUTERONOMY 29:29.

O LORD, OUR GOD, we pray for guidance, day by day, step by step, not asking nor desiring to see the distant scene. Help us to live one day at a time, knowing that the secret things, the issues of the future, belong unto God, but the things that are revealed, the unfolded issues of the day, are with us and must be met. Give us courage to face them bravely, and wisdom to handle them wisely. Our hope is in Thee. May we never turn aside from Thee to seek help from the weak and beggarly elements of the world. For Jesus' sake. *Amen.*

SILENCES OF THE SOUL

"After the fire a still small voice."
—I KINGS 19:12.

O MASTER, WE PRAY for help each day in cultivating the deep silences of the soul where God speaks. Oftentimes our lives are so noisy and disordered that we could not hear the still small voice, though it sounded long and persistently. Do Thou forgive our feverish ways and continually breathe through the heat of our desire Thy coolness and Thy balm. Teach us how to sense Thy presence, which is always near at hand and, feeling Thee ever near, may we be at peace, without and within, we ask in Thy name. *Amen.*

DAILY RENEWAL

*"They that wait upon the Lord shall renew
their strength."*—ISAIAH 40:31.

BESTOW UPON US, our Father, as
a gracious gift from above, the joy
of uninterrupted communion with
Thee. May we know, not only on the
day of the week which we endeavor
to keep sacred to Thee, but every day,
the peace and fortitude that can come
only from a conscious abiding in the
presence of God. Let this daily renewal
of our strength—yea of our very lives
—stir us to a fresh gratitude to our
Father in heaven and a more consecrated service in His church on earth.
May the lives which Christ has redeemed with His precious blood bring
forth many good works and hasten the
coming of Thy completed Kingdom. In
His name we pray. *Amen.*

DIVINE RESOURCES

1

"The king's business required haste."
—I SAMUEL 21:8.

OUR FATHER, we are grateful to Thee that the success of the gospel and the onward march of Christ's Kingdom do not depend upon such uncertain things as the interest, resources, and faithfulness of mortal and sinful men. We thank Thee for divine resources that are available for those who will use them. We rejoice in heavenly guidance and also in Thy fatherly goodness that so often overrules our mistakes and makes us advance Christ's cause even when we know it not. Yet we do pray earnestly for more consecration, less selfishness and self-seeking, more zeal to labor and more courage to be true, that the Kingdom of Glory may be hastened. In Jesus' name. *Amen.*

TRUSTING WHERE WE
CANNOT PROVE

1

"Surely the Lord is in this place; and I knew it not."—GENESIS 28:16.

O THOU, WHO DOEST all things well, we pray that after each experience of life—however dark and hard to understand—we may be able to see that Thy hand has been at work and to say: "Surely the Lord is in this place; and I knew it not." May our faith and loyalty to the things of God never be dependent on the success of our earthly plans, nor contingent on prosperity according to the standards of the world. Rather, make our fellowship with the Master utterly independent of any outward circumstances of time and space. In His name. *Amen.*

LOVE TRIUMPHANT

1

"Love worketh no ill to his neighbour: there-fore love is the fulfilling of the law."

—ROMANS 13:10.

OUR FATHER, make us believe even more firmly in the power of love, as we see hate raging rampant over the world. We are taught in Thy Word that there is a way that seemeth right to men, but the end thereof are the ways of death. Deliver us from such paths, O Lord, and turn us unto Thyself, who art the Way of Life. Help us to depend upon Thee alone who art Love Incarnate, Love Invincible, Love Triumphant. Beyond Thee we can have no hope, and in Thee do we place our trust. In Jesus' name. *Amen.*

FRUITFUL LIVES

1

"Herein is my Father glorified, that ye bear much fruit."—JOHN 15:8.

OUR FATHER, let the fullness of Thy health-giving power flow into our bodies and souls during the days that are before us. May Thy grace not be frustrated, either by our unbelief, or by our unwillingness and indifference. Help us properly to value all that life and experience bring, so that at the end of each day a conscious peace and a holy contentment may possess our souls. Thus may Thy name be glorified, and thus may our lives bear fruit, according to the promise of our Saviour. For His sake. *Amen.*

ABLER MINISTERS

"If I may but touch his garment."
—MATTHEW 9:21.

MASTER, WE THANK THEE for
the ministry of those who have been
able to touch our lives helpfully because their lives have first been touched
by Thee. Make each one of us an abler
minister of Thy grace by causing us to
be more patient bearers of Thy burden.
Whatever we may be privileged to do
in the service of our fellow men, let us
not fail in helping those to whom we
minister to become better acquainted
with Thee each day. In Thy name we
make our prayer. *Amen.*

OBLIGATION

1

"To him that knoweth to do good, and doeth it not, to him it is sin."—JAMES 4:17.

OUR LORD, we rejoice in all the high privileges that belong to us individually, as well as those that come through our Church and our nation. Surely the lines have fallen unto us in pleasant places, bringing to us a goodly heritage. May we never forget the obligations that privileges always bring. Help us to use the blessings that are ours in doing good to others. Let us never grow weary in well-doing, remembering that Thou dost never grow weary in forgiving our sins, nor in bestowing upon us Thy grace according to our needs. In the name of Him who gave Himself for us, we pray. *Amen.*

SECURITY

1

"I will fear no evil."—PSALM 23:4.

OUR FATHER, surely the multiplying tragedies of our day should impress us with the slight hold we have upon the thread of life. "So teach us to number our days, that we may apply our hearts unto wisdom." Apart from Thee we have no security, no confidence, no hope. Through faith in Thee may we lay us down and sleep, assured that if we awake on earth, God is with us, and if we awake in heaven, we are with God. Thank God for Christian faith at such a time as this. In Jesus' name. *Amen.*

COURAGE

1

"Strong in the Lord, and in the power of his might."—EPHESIANS 6:10.

W E BESEECH THEE, O God, for clearness of vision, for soundness of judgment, for courage of conviction, and for quiet confidence in Thee as we face the great problems of our time. Deliver us from an attitude of defeatism or of compromise with the forces of evil. Fill us, at needed times, with the holy indignation that the Master had when He cleansed the Temple. Imbue us with the spirit of service and sacrifice and let the peace of God which passeth understanding continually guard our minds and hearts from fear, we ask in Jesus' name. *Amen.*

THANK GOD FOR FRIENDS

"A friend loveth at all times, and a brother is born for adversity."—PROVERBS 17:17.

OUR FATHER, we thank Thee for those who have helped us along life's journey. For those who have cheered and inspired us and looked for the good in us that was often not immediately apparent, we give Thee hearty thanks. May we never withhold our help from those who are struggling and discouraged. As Thou hast blessed us so greatly, grant that we may continually strive to be a great blessing to our fellow men. In Jesus' name. *Amen.*

FACING LIFE

1

*"God hath not given us the spirit of fear; but
of power, and of love, and of a sound mind."*
—II TIMOTHY 1:7.

OUR FATHER in heaven, help us to
be utterly honest with ourselves as we
face life. Deliver us from any phase,
or form, of self-deception. May we not
be afraid to see and recognize things as
they are. Since Thou hast not given us
the spirit of fear but of power and of
love and of a sound mind, let us ever be
strong in the Lord and in the power of
His might. Make us very confident in
Thy purpose and power to cause all
things to work together for good to
them who love God. Whatever our lim-
itations may be, enable our lives,
through faith, to glorify Thee in the
service of our fellow men. In Jesus'
name. *Amen.*

AN INNER CENTER OF CALM

1

"Keep thy heart with all diligence; for out of it are the issues of life."—PROVERBS 4:23.

OUR FATHER, in the midst of the busy days, which crowd upon us with their increasing demands, grant unto us a restful spirit and a peaceful heart. May we possess an inner center of undisturbed calm and hold the preservation of this of more importance than the accomplishment of many tasks. Help us to show forth the praise of Thy grace by qualities of character, as well as by outward acts of service. In Jesus' name. *Amen.*

DISCOURAGEMENTS

1

"The Lord God is a sun and shield."
—PSALM 84:11.

O LORD, OUR GOD, we pray Thee
for courage amidst all the discourag-
ing things of life. Help us to be brave
in the face of danger, bold in the presence of the enemies of truth and righteousness, undismayed before gigantic
tasks, and filled with an unquenchable
hope, even on the darkest day. Forbid
that we should seek only the comforts
of our religion and be unwilling to face
danger, sacrifice, or death for Thy sake.
Make us very sure of the final triumph
of the cause of Him whose we are and
whom we serve. In the name of Him
who is our Sun and Shield. *Amen.*

THE SEEKING SAVIOUR

1

"There is joy in the presence of the angels of God over one sinner that repenteth."
—LUKE 15:10.

SAVIOUR, look with pity and compassion upon those of Thy children who may have slipped the anchor of their lives and are drifting aimlessly about. Draw them back to Thee with the cords of Thy tender love and anchor them again safely within the harbor of Thy grace and loving favor. Grant unto them, and unto us all, the sense of security that comes from abiding in Thee, the courage for life's tasks that is given in answer to prayer, and the unconquerable optimism that should belong to all who believe in Thee, the Lord of all life. In Thy name we make our prayer. *Amen.*

THE SENSE OF GOD

1

*"He doeth according to his will in the army
of heaven, and among the inhabitants of
the earth."*—DANIEL 4:35.

LORD, GIVE US FAITH to believe
that above the confusion of the world,
unchanged and unchangeable, affected
not at all by the passage of time, dwell-
eth the God of nations, whom we worship. Let that faith grow until we sense
amid the noise and strife of men—
pitying, forgiving, guiding, saving—
our blessed Master, who came not to be
ministered unto but to minister. Help
us each day to carry in our hearts the
sense of God transcendent, and God
close at hand; God above all earthly
things, and at the same time God ever
"treading the city streets," working
out His purposes and giving loving aid
to men. These things we ask in the
name of Him who is the same yesterday,
today, and forever. *Amen.*

ALL LOVELINESS

"O Zion; put on thy beautiful garments."
—ISAIAH 52:1.

OUR FATHER, Thou hast brought into being the world and all its beauty by the work of Thy creative hand. Create in us clean hearts, O God, and renew right spirits within us. Thou hast placed songs in the throats of birds, color in the rainbow, loveliness in a sunset scene, freshness in the breath of the morning. So make us, without and within, as Thy children, pure, lovely, attractive, joyous, and hopeful. Let the beauty of holiness, the beauty of Jesus, be seen in all those who love and trust Him, we ask in His name. *Amen.*

THE SUNSHINE OF GOD

1

"Keep yourselves in the love of God."

—JUDE 21.

OUR FATHER, so quicken our
spiritual lives that there may grow
within us, as in a soil suitable for their
culture, those precious Christian qualities of character—sympathy, helpfulness, brotherly kindness, and love. In
humbly seeking great things from Thee,
may we not be unmindful of the fact
that truly great things are not far off
but are very close to us all. Make our
own lives brighter as we try to brighten
the lives of others. May we earnestly
strive this day and always to keep ourselves in the glorious sunshine of the
unchanging love of God. These things
we ask, for Jesus' sake. *Amen.*

DEPENDABILITY

1

"Thou doest faithfully whatsoever thou doest."—III JOHN 5.

O FATHER, may we never despise nor hold lightly the quality of dependability in our work in the church and in the Kingdom. As we find this Christian grace all too rare in ourselves, as well as in our fellow servants, help us to give particular attention to its cultivation. We would be those upon whom the Lord can depend. At the same time, we would be those upon whom they can depend who have entrusted us with a sacred responsibility. Since even Christ pleased not Himself, may we not consult our own desires or convenience when duty calls, or danger. In His name. *Amen.*

FOLLOWING HIM

"I will follow thee whithersoever thou goest."
—LUKE 9:57.

GRANT to Thy followers, blessed Master, such fellowship with Thee that our lives may be continually guided as by an unseen hand. Deliver us from divided purposes and from vain regrets. May Thy spirit show forth in all our actions, and Thy love, O Christ, be the constraining, compelling motive of our service. Let there be no languor in our hearts, weakness in our words, nor weariness on our brows, as we follow Thee whithersoever Thou dost lead. In Thy name we pray. *Amen.*

THE WAY OF THE CROSS

1

*"If any man will come after me, let him deny
himself, and take up his cross."*
—MATTHEW 16:24.

DEAR LORD, we confess and ac-
knowledge that we find continual and
immediate access to Thee only because
of, and through, the sacrifice of Jesus,
Thy Son and our Saviour. Help us
to realize that a gospel of sacrifice demands sacrifice on the part of those
who would share its benefits. As Thou
dost love us, so must we love each
other. As Thou didst sacrifice for us,
so must we sacrifice for the salvation of
our fellow men. Work into the very
fiber of our souls these unchanging
Christian truths, and may the pattern
of our lives show our belief in and acceptance of them. For Jesus' sake.
Amen.

THE PURIFYING LOVE OF GOD

"Whom the Lord loveth he chasteneth."
—HEBREWS 12:6.

OUR FATHER, WE PRAY THEE to purify our zeal as Thou dost strengthen our hearts to serve Thee. May we be kept free from unworthy motives, from goals that represent personal ambition and selfish desire more than they do the glory of God, and from a spirit that wounds the Master while it professes to serve Him. Deal with us as a Father, even to harsh chastening when we offend, that we may be kept in right paths and have a conscience void of offense toward God and men. In Jesus' name. *Amen.*

COURTESY

1

"Let your moderation be known unto all men."—PHILIPPIANS 4:5.

OUR FATHER, make us able to see, to understand, and to appreciate the gentleness, the sweetness, and the consideration of our Master, Jesus Christ. Surely He is the supreme example of the highest type of courtesy, and we have all too often forgotten this in our zeal, our activity, and our self-assertiveness. Forgive the lack of this Christian grace that is sometimes painfully evident in church members. May we realize that it is just as truly our duty to be Christian gentlemen and gentlewomen as it is to possess many other qualities that have heretofore been more highly honored in the church. In Jesus' name. *Amen.*

LIGHT

1

"If . . . the light that is in thee be darkness . . . !"—MATTHEW 6:23.

THOU, who lookest upon the hearts of men, help us to face sincerely the problems that lie beneath the surface in our own lives. Having turned the light of Thy truth and holiness and love upon ourselves, may we be strong to develop those qualities of character and disposition that stand unashamed when revealed, and to cast out those that slink into darkness. Then, with victory over ourselves by Thy grace, may we help others toward victory. For Jesus' sake. *Amen.*

TRAITS OF CHARACTER

1

"The fruit of the Spirit is love, joy, peace, longsuffering, gentleness, goodness, faith, meekness, temperance: against such there is no law."—GALATIANS 5:22, 23.

OUR FATHER, forgive the faults of which we are conscious, yet will not admit even to ourselves. Help us to understand that we must frankly face life in the light of Thy truth before we can hope to be better, to feel happier, or to be rid of a sense of futility. Show us mercifully but pitilessly the character traits that we have been developing as Christians that are utterly unchristian if judged by the standards of Jesus. Help us to grow like Him in thought, word, and deed, no matter how many things dear to our selfish hearts we may have to give up. In His name. *Amen.*

HEAVENLY GIFTS

"Let not . . . your good be evil spoken of."
—ROMANS 14:16.

GRANT UNTO US, our Father, in the midst of our active service, such sweetness of spirit and such consistency of life that our friends and all who know us may find an attractiveness in our religion that will inspire them to good works. God forbid that our good should ever be evil spoken of. Make us thoughtful of others, sympathetic with their opinions even when they differ from ours, and careful always to maintain a Christian attitude toward our fellow church members. May love, unselfishness, and kindness radiate from our souls and brighten the lives of all with whom we labor. In Jesus' name. *Amen.*

A SAVIOUR FROM SIN

1

"Thou shalt call his name JESUS: for he shall save his people from their sins."
—MATTHEW 1:21.

DEAR FATHER, as we pray Thee for pardon of sins may we realize that Thou canst save us from our sins, but not in them. Help us, therefore, to face our own shortcomings rather than to seek an escape from them through excessive zeal in pious exercises. While we would keep Thy glory as the chief end of life, help us to know assuredly that nothing which hurts or degrades our brothers can possibly glorify our God, who is also their God. May Jesus, who revealed Himself as the Way, the Truth, and the Life, be incarnated in the daily lives of His followers. In His name. *Amen.*

WAITING ON THE LORD

1

*"They that wait upon the Lord shall renew
their strength."*—ISAIAH 40:31.

OUR FATHER, for the light that follows the darkness, for the sunshine
that comes after rain, for the hope
that displaces despair when we lift our
eyes heavenward, we give Thee our
grateful thanks. For the trials that
awaken within us new resources of
faith, for the challenges that stir our
sluggish hearts to new activities and
sacrifice, we bless the name of the Lord.
Forgive us our doubts and fears, which
are surely "trespasses" against Thy
love. Fill us with a new hope for each
day, and give us grace sufficient for all
life's discipline. In Jesus' name. *Amen.*

SINS OF COMPLACENCY

*"Brethren, I count not myself to have
apprehended."*—PHILIPPIANS 3:13.

OUR FATHER, deliver us from indifference in the presence of evil, complacency in the presence of human suffering, and smug satisfaction with our own spiritual life and attainments. May we never be at ease so long as large areas of our own individual lives are unsurrendered to our Lord and large areas of national and social life are unchristian. Stir us, O Lord, to constant struggle against evil and for righteousness, that Christ may be Lord of all. In His name. *Amen.*

THE BEAUTY OF PEACE

*"In the world ye shall have tribulation: but
be of good cheer."*—JOHN 16:33.

LIFT US THIS DAY, O Lord, above
the strife and sin of the streets into the
calm, clear atmosphere of communion
with, and peace in, Thee. "Take from
our souls the strain and stress, and let
our ordered lives confess the beauty of
Thy peace." Having been thus refreshed, let us then face the tasks and
take up the burdens of life without fear
or anxiety, and with gladness and sin-
gleness of heart. Make our lives count
from day to day, not only in things
done, but in the quality of spirit we
possess when things go wrong and the
road seems rough. In Jesus' name.
Amen.

THY PERFECT PLAN

1

*"O the depth of the riches both of the wisdom
and knowledge of God!"*—ROMANS 11:33.

O GOD, WE THANK THEE for the experiences of life that show us the depths of Thy wisdom and the greatness of Thy love for men. We are glad that even our importunate prayers do not turn Thee aside from Thy perfect plan, and we trust that prayer and communion may continually keep us in harmony with these plans. Graciously pardon our sins of ignorance, willfulness, and selfishness. Purify us by Thine indwelling Spirit, and grant that we may use the talents and power given unto us, as well as the wealth and possessions, in the great Kingdom program of our God. In Jesus' name. *Amen.*

THE GOODNESS OF GOD

"I shall not want."—PSALM 23:1.

WE THANK THEE, dear Lord, for the gracious way Thou dost restore the creatures of Thy hand when life and conditions and things seem to be dealing too harshly with them. To the parched, dry earth the summer showers come with gentle refreshment. To the weary, discouraged souls of men come the still dews of God's grace. May we never doubt Thy goodness, nor feel that Thy love has forsaken us. Let us know in our hearts that God is ever in the midst of His people, God is ever at the right hand of His child, and God will supply every need of ours according to His riches in glory. Praised be Thy name! *Amen.*

GROWTH IN GRACE

1

*"Despisest thou the riches of his goodness and
forbearance and longsuffering . . . ?"*
—ROMANS 2:4.

OUR FATHER, with our hearts as
well as our voices, we praise and thank
Thee for the love of God which passeth knowledge, a love which we can
grow to know better only as we experience it and love Thee in return. We
are grateful for Thine infinite patience,
for Thy never-failing mercy, and for
the kindness which Thou dost show us,
even when we are unkind to our fellow
men and ungrateful to Thee. Help us
to grow each day in grace, and thus become more Christlike in all our ways.
God forbid that we should be among
those who despise the riches of Thy
goodness, forbearance, and long-suffering, we humbly pray in Jesus' name.
Amen.

THE FRUIT OF THE SPIRIT

"The letter killeth, but the spirit giveth life."
—II CORINTHIANS 3:6.

W E BESEECH THEE, O GOD, to overrule our mistakes and to strengthen us in all that is good. Cause the fruit of the Spirit to be produced in great abundance in the life of the church, as well as in the life of each Christian. If we find any lack of love, joy, peace, long-suffering, gentleness, goodness, faith, meekness, temperance in ourselves, make us dissatisfied with everything else we may seem to have accomplished in the Christian life. May Christians become more Christlike and the church more unified as we struggle against evil and for the right. In Jesus' name. *Amen.*

MORE CHRISTIAN

1

"Lest that by any means, when I have preached to others, I myself should be a castaway."
—I Corinthians 9:27.

O GOD, MAKE US more Christian in our zeal for Christianity, more universal in our love and application of the gospel's saving power, more unselfish in the things we do in the church. God forbid that when we have ministered to others we should ourselves be cast away because of cherished sins, or sinful attitudes, feelings, and thoughts, which we have refused to give up. We pray in Jesus' name. *Amen.*

SINNERS, NOT THE RIGHTEOUS

1

"Let us lay aside every weight, and the sin which doth so easily beset us."

—HEBREWS 12:1.

OUR FATHER, we come to Thee in the name of Jesus, who, though sinless, has known all man's infirmities. Look with pity upon us—our weakness, our purposelessness, our failures, and our besetting sins. Help us to believe that it was sinners, not the righteous, whom Jesus came to save and that He is able to save each one of us, even the chief of sinners. Make our belief so strong that we shall be willing to let go our own most-cherished plans and to lay aside our besetting sins that God may rule our lives—rule supreme and rule alone. For Jesus' sake. *Amen.*

FRIENDS

1

*"There is a friend that sticketh closer than
a brother."*—PROVERBS 18:24.

OUR FATHER, we thank Thee for
friends who believe in us and pray
for us—friends whose faith in us
makes us better than we otherwise
would be. We rejoice in all the opportunities that come to us for showing
Christian friendship. Put it into our
hearts to make one of the most earnest
efforts of our Christian lives that of being friends to those in need and better
friends to those whose lives we touch
in Christian service. For Jesus' sake.
Amen.

FULFILLMENT

1

"Their soul shall be as a watered garden."
—JEREMIAH 31:12.

THANKS BE UNTO THEE, our Maker
and Redeemer, for Thy goodness and
mercy which never fail. Create in
us grateful hearts, and renew a thankful spirit within Thy people. Let not
the passing pleasures of the hour, nor
the heavy burdens of the moment,
dim our gratitude to Thee nor make
us careless or resentful. In Thee alone
can be found fulfillment of the unsatisfied yearnings of the soul. May we
never seek elsewhere for that blessedness
which is always close at hand in the
blessed presence of God. In the name of
Him who can make our souls become
as watered gardens. *Amen.*

THE NARROW WAY

1

*"Strait is the gate, and narrow is the way,
which leadeth unto life."*—MATTHEW 7:14.

O CHRIST OF THE NARROW WAY,
keep Thy children from being so absorbed in the material things of the
world that they begin to neglect spiritual realities. Surely love, joy, and
peace should mean more to men made
in the image of God than riches, position, and prominence. Forgive us when
we turn aside from the path we should
follow to seek the sinful attractions of
the world. Draw us back to the way
that leads to life, and ever save us by
Thy grace from sin that dwells in us, as
well as sin that is on every side. In Thy
name we pray. *Amen.*

TOWARD SUNSET

"The hoary head is a crown of glory."
—PROVERBS 16:31.

WE THANK THEE, OUR MASTER, for lives that have been lived in the fear, as well as in the service, of God. Surely a hoary head is a crown of glory if it be found in the way of righteousness. Help us to live day by day so unselfishly, so purposefully, and so nobly that we shall be a blessing to others as we near the end of the journey and see the sun beginning to set. When we are no longer able to be active and busy about many things, may our lives be a benediction through what we have grown to be in the friendship and service of God. In Thy name. *Amen.*

CROSSES AND CROWNS

"If we suffer, we shall also reign with him."
—II TIMOTHY 2:12.

OUR FATHER, impart unto our troubled spirits something of the calmness that pervaded the life of our Master. We have sought the majesty of possessions and power in earthly things and our souls have been unsatisfied. We long for the majestic sweetness that sits enthroned upon the Saviour's brow. Direct our search, our struggles, and our work along paths that lead to spiritual likeness to the Master, even though these paths may take us where crosses are better known than crowns. In His name. *Amen.*

LOVE WAITING

1

"I will arise and go to my father."
—LUKE 15:18.

O LORD, Thou art our God and hast been the dwelling place of Thy people in all generations. Make us realize that, in so far as we live and move and consciously have our being in Thee, we are kept safe from the evils of the world. May we early learn that apart from Thee we cannot fulfill our mission in the world, nor can we experience joy and satisfaction in life. Grant to us both the desire and the ability to arise from the cramped and limited quarters of self and selfishness, where we have dwelt too long, into the fullness of God, who is our Father, and who is waiting with extended arms for the return of every straying, prodigal son. In Jesus' name. *Amen.*

DOERS OF THE WORD
1

"By their fruits ye shall know them."
—MATTHEW 7:20.

OUR FATHER, cause us to show by outward acts of service the fruits of an inner grace. May our righteousness exceed the righteousness of the scribes and Pharisees. May our love, unselfishness, liberality, and sacrifice put to shame the sordid greed of the world. As a tree is known by its fruits, so we pray that our lives may be known by the good works that they bring forth. Help us to be doers of the word and not hearers only, we ask for Jesus' sake. *Amen.*

ENCOURAGEMENT

1

"By the good hand of our God upon us."
—EZRA 8:18.

WE ARE GRATEFUL to Thee, Eternal God, whose almighty hand controls the years, that Thou dost guide Thy children along the difficult and lengthening paths of life. Grant us the joy and satisfaction, as we look back over the years from time to time, of seeing clearly that the good hand of God has ever been upon us. Thus strengthened and encouraged, may we then look forward with confidence and cheerfully take up again the tasks that are ours. For Jesus' sake. *Amen.*

SWEETNESS OF SPIRIT

"When he was reviled, [he] reviled not again."—I PETER 2:23.

CREATE IN US clean hearts, O God, and renew right spirits within us. Make us valiant champions of the right and uncompromising foes of the wrong. As we work and struggle, as we succeed and fail, as we rejoice and sorrow, may we always have a sweetness of spirit and an unconquerable belief in the final triumph of all that is good. Thus may men take knowledge of us that we have been with Thee in the secret places and that we are Thine. In the dear Saviour's name we pray. *Amen.*

STABILIZING POWER

"In him all things hold together." *
—COLOSSIANS 1:17.

W E THANK THEE, our heavenly Father, for the stabilizing power of the gospel of Christ in both men and nations, even those unyielded to Him. In and through our Saviour and Lord, the universe exists as a harmonious whole. Make us realize that in proportion as we give ourselves, our interest, our time, and our money to the work of Christ through the church, in that proportion both harmony and security will be advanced and Christ's Kingdom be brought nearer its final completion. For His sake. *Amen.*

---

*Marginal reading of American Standard Version.

CO-WORKERS

1

"Whatsoever a man soweth, that shall he also reap."—GALATIANS 6:7.

OUR FATHER, as we cannot deceive Thee in our offerings, make us to know that we cannot outgive Thee when we bring our gifts to Thy altar. Help us to be utterly sincere and honest with ourselves, as we profess to be honest with Thee, in setting aside a due proportion of our possessions for Kingdom work. Surely, in the very acceptance of our offerings by Thee we are blessed, and in the privilege of making an offering we are honored by becoming co-workers with God. Grant that we may sow to the Spirit, that we of the Spirit may reap life everlasting. In Jesus' name. *Amen.*

"ABIDE WITH ME"

"Jesus Christ the same yesterday, and to day, and for ever."—HEBREWS 13:8.

IN THE MIDST of time, our Father, we pray to Thee who art timeless. Faced by change and decay in all things around, we turn toward Thee who art changeless, the same yesterday, today, and forever. Confronted by forces and powers that are sinister and evil, we find our courage and our help in the Lord who made heaven and earth. Fill us with Thyself this day, that our hearts may become strong, our courage renewed, and our lives made purposeful and happy, we pray in Jesus' name. *Amen.*

FINAL VICTORY

*"He which hath begun a good work in you
will perform it until the day of Jesus Christ."*
—PHILIPPIANS 1:6.

OUR FATHER, grant unto us, in the
presence of all the threatening dan-
gers and present uncertainties of life, a
sense of security coming from our faith
in God. May we never doubt His ultimate purposes of redemption and the
final victory of the spiritual forces of
righteousness and truth. Keep us from
indifference, as well as overconfidence,
in our religion. Grant that we may be
patient in trial, courageous in service,
and continuous in prayer as life goes
forward, we ask for Jesus' sake. *Amen.*

THE PATIENCE OF GOD

1

*"He hath not dealt with us after our sins; nor
rewarded us according to our iniquities."*
—PSALM 103:10.

O MASTER, in the midst of the noise
and confusion of life, give us patient spirits and hearts full of sympathy. Help us to understand what things
of the world are real and abiding, and
to think more on these things. May we
give less time to those things that last
but for a moment and are gone. If our
own hearts are sad, let us find relief
in comforting the hearts of others that
may be still sadder. If we tend to grow
impatient may we consider the patience
of God, who has ever dealt with us in
our willfulness with love and forbearance. For Jesus' sake. *Amen.*

STALWART FAITH

1

*"The Spirit of the Lord clothed himself with
Gideon."**—JUDGES 6:34.

BLESSED BE THE LORD for His
strong Spirit, who has clothed Himself
with His servants that yield themselves
to do His will. We rejoice in the stal-
wart faith, the unswerving courage,
and the sacrificial spirit of our mission-
aries at home and abroad. We commend
to Thee for a fresh enduement of grace
those who struggle against mighty foes
and spiritual wickedness. We pray for
a deeper consecration and a willingness
to suffer among us all, who may be tried
as by fire in the days ahead. In Jesus'
name. *Amen.*

---

*Translation from the Hebrew.

PATIENCE

1

*"In your patience ye shall win your souls."**
—LUKE 21:19.

GIVE US PATIENCE as we await
the long, long processes of God, we
pray Thee, our heavenly Father. Give
us endurance and fortitude as we watch
evil apparently becoming stronger and
see such little results from our efforts
in the cause of righteousness and truth
and peace. Help us to trust Thee more
implicitly and, at the same time, to be
more earnest and faithful in our Christian life and service. In our steadfast-
ness and patience may our souls grow
strong. In Jesus' name. *Amen.*

---

*American Standard Version. Marginal reading: "In
your stedfastness ye shall win your lives."

USING EVERY OCCASION

"Without me ye can do nothing."
—JOHN 15:5.

O LORD OUR GOD, encourage us ever in our struggles against sin by the consciousness of the presence of the undaunted Saviour. May we continually have within us a vision of Him who made every experience an occasion of helpful service; who was in command of every situation, even when being scourged and crucified; and who ever liveth to give victory to His faithful followers. May we, with Paul, be able to do all things through Christ who strengtheneth us. In His name. *Amen.*

ETERNAL SPRINGTIME

"Let not your heart be troubled."
—JOHN 14:1.

SPIRIT OF GOD, descend upon our hearts and make them sing with the gladness of eternal springtime, even in the midst of the darkest winter of trial and sorrow. Breathe peace and comfort and strength into the lives of all God's children who faint and grow weary. Guide our stumbling feet into pastures of tender greenness and beside still waters of refreshment. Glorify the name of the Lord in lives redeemed by His grace, making them shine more brightly as shadows grow darker. May all who are Thine be led to seek continually Thy guidance as they look toward, and plan for, the things that lie ahead. In Jesus' name. *Amen.*

CLOSE TO THEE

1

"Draw nigh to God, and he will draw nigh to you."—JAMES 4:8.

As we trust in Thee alone for eternal salvation, our Saviour, so we look to Thee for grace to live our present lives. Too often we follow Thee afar off and our hearts become cold, our souls lean. Draw us so close to Thee that we may be partakers of Thy grace and be ready, when Thou willest, to be sharers of Thy suffering and then of Thy glory. Let Thy Spirit cease not His strivings within us until we yield to Him without reserve and become true followers of God, as dear children. In Thy name we pray. *Amen.*

NEW CREATURES

*"If any man be in Christ, he is a new
creature."*—II CORINTHIANS 5:17.

OUR FATHER, scatter the still dews
of Thy quietness upon all troubled
hearts, this day. Refresh the wearied lives of those whose burdens are
heavy. Release the tension that is found
in too many of us and that tires us out
without accomplishing anything that
is satisfying or abiding. Give life a new
meaning, suffering a new hallowing influence, and sorrow a new purifying
power, that we may indeed be new creatures in Christ through our faith in
Him. In His name we pray. *Amen.*

HE KNOWS BEST

*"All things work together for good to them
that love God."*—ROMANS 8:28.

HELP US, DEAR SAVIOUR, to believe
in our hearts that God who made us
and redeemed us from sin and death
knows what is best for us in this life.
In the presence of experiences that are
both baffling and bewildering, may we
not doubt Thy wisdom and Thy love.
Give us strength to obey Thy com-
mands, so that happiness may replace
unhappiness in our lives and fruitful-
ness crowd out futility. May we bear
Thy burdens, as well as do Thy work,
joyfully. In Thy name we pray. *Amen.*

CONFIDENCE

1

"God is our refuge and strength."
—PSALM 46:1.

OUR FATHER, though we may not be always conscious of Thy presence in our lives, yet as we look over the days passed by, we can see that Thou hast always been with us. Grant that a holy confidence born of experience of Thee, even when we knew not it was Thee, may enable us to face the tasks of the present and the uncertainty of the future unafraid. Thou who hast been with us art with us today and wilt continue to be our Refuge and Strength through all the days to come. In this assurance, let us always rejoice. In Jesus' name. *Amen.*

EVERY NEED SUPPLIED

1

"My God shall supply every need of yours." *
—PHILIPPIANS 4:19.

WE WORSHIP and praise Thee, Creator of all things and Giver of every good and perfect gift. Thou openest Thine hand and suppliest the needs of all men. Help us to have more faith and trust in Thine uninterrupted goodness and Thine unchanging watch over Thy children. Deliver us from fear and from all dread of the future. Make us willing to leave in Thy hands the unknown things ahead. At the same time, we pray that we may be stirred to continual faithfulness in Thy service and unswerving loyalty to Thy cause. For Jesus' sake. *Amen.*

---

*American Standard Version.

AS LITTLE CHILDREN

"Except ye turn, and become as little children, ye shall in no wise enter into the kingdom."
—MATTHEW 18:3.*

WE THANK THEE, dear Master, for those forces and influences in our lives that guided us aright when we were incapable of guiding ourselves. We bless Thee for our parents, for the friends of our youth, and for all those whose sympathy and helpfulness strengthened us during the years of immaturity. May we all continually remain as little children in the presence of God and daily seek direction for our steps as a child seeks direction from his parents, we ask in Thy name. *Amen.*

*American Standard Version.

BEAUTY

*"And God saw every thing that he had made,
and, behold, it was very good."*
—GENESIS 1:31

OUR FATHER, may we ever sense
behind and beyond the beautiful things
of the world the ineffable loveliness
of Him who created them. Let the
beauty of a spring day, the pure melody
of a singing bird, the deep blue of a
baby's eyes, the lilting laughter of an
innocent child, the unruffled calmness
on the face of one grown old in Thy
service, make real to us the beauty of
the Lord, our Maker, and the tender
kindness of God, our heavenly Father.
Surely Thy ways are ways of pleasant-
ness and all Thy paths are peace. *Amen.*

SECURE

1

"The foundation of God standeth sure."
—II TIMOTHY 2:19.

WE TURN OUR EYES, wearied with the changing things of earth, to Thee, who changest not. We rest our minds, harassed and troubled by the uncertainties of time, on Thee, who art eternally the same. We anchor our souls, oppressed by the sin and weakness of mortal flesh, in the haven of Thy mercy, Thy loving-kindness, and Thy forgiveness. May we be confident and unafraid, however dark and distressing our experiences may seem to be, since Thou art our God and Father. Let Thy discipline purify us, Thy love uphold us, and Thy purposes ever be uppermost in our minds and hearts. In Jesus' name. *Amen.*

"THE STEPS OF A GOOD MAN"

"The steps of a good man are ordered by the Lord."—PSALM 37:23.

OUR FATHER, in the presence of increasing evil, which is everywhere existent in the world, make us more confident of, as well as dependent upon, the triumphant power of Christ, the Conqueror of death and hell. Realizing that "it is not in man that walketh to direct his steps," may we believe firmly that the steps of a good man may always be ordered of the Lord. Through the winding paths of life lead us onward, we pray, with our eyes ever fixed on the goal at the end of the way and our hands ever conscious of the touch of His hand on ours. In Jesus' name. *Amen.*

FEAR

1

"There is no fear in love."—I JOHN 4:18.

W E LIFT UP our hearts and voices in praise and gratitude to Thee, O God, who hast provided eternal life for all who will accept Christ as their Saviour. Take fear out of our hearts and give us confidence and joy in our religion. May our lives, lived through faith in Christ, commend our Saviour to others. May our lips, cleansed by Thy grace, tell the glad gospel story to those who know it not. We pray in the name of Him whose perfect love casteth out fear. *Amen.*

FELLOWSHIP

1

"And they continued stedfastly in the apostles' doctrine and fellowship."

—ACTS 2:42.

GRANT UNTO US, we do pray Thee, O Lord, loving hearts that shall always be quick to help and sympathize and slow to criticize or hurt. Bind Thy people together with ties of conscious unity, so that a fellowship of love and a warm human understanding may readily be found in their associations with each other at whatever point of church life they may touch. May we be utterly sincere, entirely devoid of selfishness, and wholly open to the warm inflooding experience of the Holy Spirit. In Jesus' name. *Amen.*

VESSELS UNTO HONOR

"Create in me a clean heart. O God; and renew a right spirit within me."—PSALM 51:10.

OUR HOPE IS IN THEE, eternal God, both in life and in death. Do Thou convince us that the greatest human resources of mortal man are not sufficient for the needs of this life and cannot even touch the life to come. Reveal unto us our increasing need and Thy power to supply that need. Then, make us just as willing to receive and use this power as Thou art willing to bestow it. Cleanse our hearts and lives of those things that hinder and interrupt the work of the Holy Spirit and make of us both vessels and channels of living water, sanctified and meet for the Master's use. In His name. *Amen.*

FAITH

"Lord, Increase our faith."—LUKE 17:5.

WE PRAY THEE, Master, to increase our faith in Thee as we start out on the duties of the day and, at the same time, to increase our faith in our fellow men. Make us realize that without faith it is impossible to please God, to please ourselves, or to please anyone else. Since the man with the largest faith is the man who lives the fullest life, make our faith grow day by day, whatever else may be denied us. In Thy name we pray. *Amen.*

ENDURING HARDNESS

"The disciple is not above his master, nor the servant above his lord."—MATTHEW 10:24.

OUR FATHER, we thank Thee for the times in our life's experience when we are forced so utterly up against reality that the shams and superficialities which have hitherto deceived us fall away. Surely it is through enduring hardness as a good soldier of Jesus Christ that we understand mysteries which are hidden from those who live easily and complacently. Teach us that it is often under the burden of a great sorrow we can feel most truly the strength of the everlasting arms. May we understand when our own resources are exhausted that it is then we find most surely the exhaustless resources of God. For such wisdom, which is hidden from our eyes until revealed by Thee, we are humbly grateful. In Jesus' name. *Amen.*

THE SIGNS OF THE TIMES

"If any of you lack wisdom, let him ask of God, that giveth to all men liberally."

—JAMES 1:5.

O THOU WHO ART THE WAY, the Truth, and the Life, we pray for wisdom to discern the signs of the times that we may know what God's spiritual Israel ought to do. Keep us ever from confusing our own selfish wants and ambitions with the will of the Lord. God forbid that we should identify the progress of Thy Kingdom with the maintenance of institutions which violate the spirit of Thy gospel or with the progress of social panaceas which are only time-serving. Help us to give ourselves to the things that are eternal and to be concerned about those things that will last when we are gone. For Jesus' sake. *Amen.*

SANE AND BALANCED

"For we walk by faith, not by sight."
—II CORINTHIANS 5:7.

OUR FATHER, make our faith grow stronger as the years pass and we realize, more and more, that we must walk by faith, rather than by sight. Help us to depend on Thee for necessary things, at the same time using to the fullest the ways and means given unto us for procuring these things. In the midst of an unbalanced and insane world, keep Thy people sane and balanced, lest we ourselves miss the way and hinder, rather than help, in our efforts to serve God. In Jesus' name. *Amen.*

COURAGE PLUS HUMILITY

*"Who went about doing good, and healing
all that were oppressed of the devil."*
—ACTS 10:38.

GIVE US, O GOD, a courageous
spirit in our fight for the right and a
humble spirit in our dealings with
those who do not see as we do, nor
fight in the same manner. May we ever
be saved from the sin of confusing our
own desires with the will of God by
constantly testing them at the eternal
standard of Christ's teachings and example. Help us to do with our might
the things our hands find to do. And
grant that the power of love and the
resistless force of selflessness and sacrifice may always be pre-eminent qualities of whatever might we possess. In
Jesus' name. *Amen.*

HELPING EACH OTHER

"If ye forgive not men their trespasses . . ."
—MATTHEW 6:15.

O LORD, MAKE US those who seek to encourage our brethren. May we be helpful rather than fault-finding. Since we trust that Thou wilt forgive our trespasses, so may we gladly forgive the trespasses of our fellow men. Fill us with a yearning desire to do all we can to make the sinful world a better place by being more Christlike ourselves and helping others to be better. In Jesus' name. *Amen.*

BRIGHTNESS

1

"The entrance of thy words giveth light."
—PSALM 119:130.

OUR FATHER, brighten with the smile of Thy countenance the hearts of Thy children who look upward to seek Thy face this day. May each of us find in Thee not only the complete fulfillment of our deepest spiritual desires, but also new and deeper desires and a fuller meaning of Thy salvation. As we learn more of the ways of God from a closer study of the Holy Scriptures, may our experience be that of the Psalmist of old, that the entrance of Thy words giveth light. In the name of Him who is the Light of the world. *Amen.*

THE SET OF THE HEART

1

*"For Ezra had set his heart to seek the law of
Jehovah."* *——EZRA 7:10.

MASTER, GIVE US wisdom to
know the right, courage to choose it,
and strength to do it. May our hearts
be inclined toward all things pure and
true, our minds be disciplined by
thoughts noble and good, and our
strength exercised always to fight
against evil and for right. Let us be so
yielded to God's Spirit through the
years that our lives will count mightily
in the work of Thy Kingdom. We long
for Thee to be able to depend on us in
all Thou givest us to do. In Thy name
we pray. *Amen.*

*American Standard Version.

OUR THOUGHTS

"As he thinketh in his heart, so is he."
—PROVERBS 23:7.

OUR HEAVENLY FATHER, we need Thy help every hour in our struggle to keep our thoughts clean and pure. May we never forget that what a man does outwardly has already been done in his heart. Forbid that we should ever allow to remain unchallenged within us thoughts that are unkind, impure, or sinful. Teach us how to drive that which is evil out of our minds by keeping them continually at work thinking upon things that are high and holy, upon those things that are in keeping with our thoughts of Jesus. In His name. *Amen.*

MEMORIES

1

*"I thank my God upon every remembrance of
you."*—PHILIPPIANS 1:3.

WE ARE GRATEFUL, dear Lord, for
the beautiful memories that are ours.
Especially do we thank Thee upon
every remembrance of those who have
touched our lives and made us better.
For those who have inspired us, who
believed in us, and who helped us when
we were too weak, too immature, or
too foolish to help ourselves, we praise
Thy name. We would make it one of
the purposes of our lives to be such
friends to others that some one of them
may thank God when he calls us to
mind. For Jesus' sake. *Amen.*

SACRIFICE

"He that loseth his life for my sake shall find it."—MATTHEW 10:39.

OUR MASTER, help us to see clearly and to decide wisely when we are faced with a choice between the way of self-seeking and the way of self-sacrifice. May the example of Jesus' life inspire us and the triumph of His death empower us to follow in His footsteps wherever they may lead. Make us willing to lose our lives in service and sacrifice that we may find them again gloriously perfected in Christ, our Saviour. In Him we would live now and eternally. *Amen.*

TRIUMPHANT TO THE END

"He that endureth to the end shall be saved."
—MATTHEW 10:22.

ETERNAL GOD, blessed be Thy name for the faith that brings us safely through life to its end and carries us triumphantly to our heavenly home. Blessed be Thy name for the faith that enables us to look up and continue to live and labor when those we love are called from us unto Thee. Blessed be the name of the Lord for making provision for every need of His children both in this life and the life to come. *Amen and Amen!*

PRAYERS

FOR SPECIAL DAYS

THE LORD'S DAY

"I was in the Spirit on the Lord's day."
—REVELATION 1:10.

OUR FATHER IN HEAVEN, we pray Thee to lift us up in spirit this Lord's day morning from the sinful and confusing things of earth unto realms of peace and communion with Thee. During the week past we have too often sought happiness and satisfaction from the things of the world and found them not. Disappointed on every hand, thwarted on every side, ladened with the burden of sin, we turn to Thee as the flower turns for its life and beauty and fragrance to the sun overhead. As we worship Thee at home, in our church, or elsewhere may the peace of Him who promised to be with us all the days satisfy our every need. In His name. *Amen.*

NEW YEAR

1

"A thousand years in thy sight are but as yesterday when it is past."—PSALM 90:4.

O GOD, at the beginning of a division of time which men call years, we rejoice to worship a God to whom time does not apply. Thou art the same, yesterday, today, and forever, without beginning of days or end of years. Thou knowest the end from the beginning, and from ancient times the things which are not yet done. Because Thou art not only timeless in Thy being, but art merciful and gracious, slow to anger and plenteous in mercy, we would slip our hands into Thine and set forth fearlessly, joyously, upon the unknown and untrodden path of the New Year. In Jesus' name. *Amen.*

NEW YEAR

1

"The days of our years."——PSALM 90:10.

LORD, let the glorious gift of a new year with days unspotted refresh our spirits during this week. May no fear of things unseen nor dread of the future mar the joy of the beginning of our journey. Give us the confidence that the same God who was with the Psalmist all the days of his life will surely be with His children all the days of this year. In this confidence and with a renewed consecration, may we set forth, courageously and unafraid, to do the will of God as He reveals it to us day by day. For Jesus' sake. *Amen.*

NEW YEAR

"The eternal God is thy refuge."
—DEUTERONOMY 33:27.

THOU WHO ART, from everlasting to everlasting, God, be with us as we enter the new year. Thou, who knowest the end from the beginning, guide us through the perplexing paths ahead. Thou, who remainest unchanged, stablish our hearts and strengthen our wills as we set forth upon the days allotted unto us. Thou, whose years do not fail, work in us an unchanging and unchangeable faith so that, in the midst of time, we may live, like Thee, in Eternity. And to Thee be glory, by Christ Jesus, in the church and in our lives, forevermore. *Amen.*

EASTER

"He rose again the third day."
—I CORINTHIANS 15:4.

OUR HEAVENLY FATHER, we thank Thee for Christ, our Saviour, who hath abolished death and brought life and immortality to light through the gospel. As He was delivered for our transgressions and rose again for our justification, so may we walk continuously in newness of life. Help us not only at this season of the year but every day to live without fear, in perfect peace and confident faith in Him who for our sakes died and rose again. In His name, we ask it. *Amen.*

EASTER

"We also should walk in newness of life."
—ROMANS 6:4.

DEAR LORD, as we rejoice and sing praises to Thee at this Resurrection season, grant that Christ may rise again in every heart where He has been entombed. May He become a living Saviour, the vital force and directing power in the church and in the personal lives of His followers. In the world that now knows Him not, may His grace restrain the forces of evil and strengthen the forces of righteousness. Our hope is in Him alone and only through Him can victory come. In the only name under heaven given among men whereby we must be saved, we make our prayer. *Amen.*

EASTER

"That I may know him, and the power of his resurrection."—PHILIPPIANS 3:10.

O GOD, may the power for Christian living, released in the world by the glorious resurrection of our Lord, be felt in the lives of all Thy children. Not only at the Easter season, but every day, cause our hearts to be bright with the undimmed light that shines through the centuries from the open tomb, out of which the Master came forth in newness of life. Let no redeemed child of God live in darkness, or gloom, or sin, but may all who are called by Thy name keep themselves in the glorious light of Thy love. For Jesus' sake. *Amen.*

MOTHER'S DAY

"A mother in Israel."—JUDGES 5:7.

O GOD, we thank Thee for mothers in Thy spiritual Israel who rear their children in the fear of God, which is the beginning of wisdom. Increase their number in our midst, O Lord! Make it the ambition of every mother who follows our Master to train her children so well in the principles of Christianity that these children may be better Christians than their parents. Let no Christian mother be turned aside from her high, God-given duty and privilege by the allurements of the world or by the desire that her children prosper in temporal rather than eternal things. In Jesus' name. *Amen.*

MOTHER'S DAY

"And the child grew, and waxed strong in spirit, filled with wisdom."—LUKE 2:40.

OUR FATHER, we are grateful to Thee for all the blessed influences that entered into our lives when we were young. We thank Thee, also, for the things that have remained with us through life, making us better, truer, nobler. The Lord be praised for all Christian parents whose earnest aim and effort has been the rearing of their children into fine, Christian manhood and womanhood. May those of us who are parents today let nothing take precedence over this God-given duty and privilege, and grant us good success in our efforts here whatever failures may attend elsewhere. In Jesus' name. *Amen.*

MOTHER'S DAY

1

*"The unfeigned faith . . . which dwelt first
in thy grandmother Lois, and thy mother
Eunice."*—II TIMOTHY 1:5.

OUR FATHER, our hearts go out
in gratitude to Thee for Christian
mothers and the unfeigned faith which
dwells in so many of them. We bless
Thy name for the sacred memories of
our mothers who have been called
home to Thee, and for the influence of
their love which still remains with us.
Help us, today and every day, to honor
and cherish the true, the precious, and
the noble things of life. We thank Thee
that our mothers symbolize these things
for many of us, realizing that in Jesus
alone can we find them perfectly incarnated. As we thank Thee for our
mothers, we thank Thee most of all
for the gift of Thy Son. In His name.
Amen.

INDEPENDENCE DAY

1

*"He doeth according to his will in the army
of heaven, and among the inhabitants of
the earth."*—DANIEL 4:35.

OUR FATHER IN HEAVEN, as the
season has come again for the celebra-
tion of our national birthday, may we
remember and meditate upon the words
of Scripture that declare: "Blessed is the
nation whose God is the Lord." Turn
the hearts of the leaders of our nation,
as well as the hearts of individual citizens, to Thee who doest Thy will in
the army of heaven and among the inhabitants of earth. May the church of
Christ ever stand as a lighthouse among
the nations of the earth. We pray Thee
to dispel the darkness that has grown
very dense in the world and bring to
us all a new hope of peace on earth,
good will to men. In Jesus' name.
Amen.

INDEPENDENCE DAY

"Righteousness exalteth a nation: but sin is a reproach to any people."—PROVERBS 14:34.

O GOD, we feel very grateful to Thee for Thy goodness to us as we celebrate the birthday of our nation. Yet we would be very humble when we think of our carelessness and indifference to the things that be of God. "Lord God of Hosts, be with us yet, lest we forget—lest we forget!" Send forth a spirit of humility and repentance into the hearts of our citizens this day. Help us to turn from broken cisterns that hold no water to the Fountain of Water that springs up into everlasting life—to Thee—the living and true God. From Thee alone can come times of refreshing and streams of healing. Send them upon us, O Lord, we humbly beseech Thee. In Jesus' name. *Amen.*

LABOR DAY

1

"Is not this the carpenter, the son of Mary?"
—MARK 6:3.

OUR FATHER GOD, as Thou didst find the highest expression of Thyself on earth in the person and life of a man of labor, a carpenter, so teach us the duty and the dignity of labor. May we early discover that only in the best performance of every task which is ours can we find true happiness and peace of mind. And may those of our fellows who toil with their hands that we may be comfortable and protected ever receive our brotherly affection and our sincere good will. In the name of Jesus. *Amen.*

LABOR DAY

"Even as the Son of man came not to be ministered unto, but to minister."

—MATTHEW 20:28.

O GOD, we rejoice that Jesus labored among men, ministering to others in need. We thank Thee that throughout the centuries He has ever been the friend of those who labor with their hands. We beseech Thee to forgive Thy people whenever and wherever they show themselves unfriendly to, or unsympathetic with, those who labor. Make us realize that in the Kingdom of God there are no positions of preferment that are not gained by labor and service to others. Help us, therefore, rather than being conformed to the world to be transformed by the renewing of our minds, so that we may show forth in our lives the things which are good and acceptable to God, as revealed in Christ. For His sake. *Amen.*

THANKSGIVING

1

*"In every thing by prayer and supplication
with thanksgiving."*—PHILIPPIANS 4:6.

OUR FATHER, we give thanks to
Thee for the blessings that come to us
during all the days of the year. We
thank Thee for the joys that brighten
our lives and the sorrows that discipline
our spirits. We thank Thee for the
friends who have helped us bear the
burdens of life and whose faith in us
has spurred us on to harder efforts and
higher purpose. We thank Thee for the
kindly ministries of the church and for
the opportunities of service to others
that the church offers. And we thank
Thee most of all for Jesus, our Master
and Lord, whose gentle Spirit has led
captive our rebellious spirits and whose
gospel is our strong hope for time and
eternity. In His name. *Amen.*

THANKSGIVING

1

"Though he was rich, yet for your sakes he became poor."—II CORINTHIANS 8:9.

O GIVER of every good and perfect gift, may the richness of Thy blessings be met by the deep and sincere gratitude of Thy children. Help us to be thankful in everyday life, bringing forth the fruits of thanksgiving in ministering to others for our Master's sake. As Thou wast touched with the feeling of our infirmities, so may we be touched by all suffering, poverty, and distress among our fellow men. Let us rejoice to minister to those in need, remembering the unstinted ministry of our Saviour, "who went about doing good, and healing all that were oppressed." In His name. *Amen.*

THANKSGIVING

1

"I will bless the Lord at all times."
—PSALM 34:1.

OUR CREATOR AND GOD, **breathe a** spirit of thanksgiving into the hearts of all Thy people throughout this week. May those to whom life has seemed hard have revealed to them many causes for rejoicing that hitherto they have not seen. May those who are the more fortunate of the world rejoice in the service they can render to their fellow man. And may we all rejoice in the fellowship that Christian brethren can have with each other and with our Lord, whatever the outward circumstances of life may be. For Jesus' sake. *Amen.*

CHRISTMAS

"Unto you is born this day in the city of David a Saviour."—LUKE 2:11.

OUR HEAVENLY FATHER, as the Christmas season approaches our hearts soften in the glow of love that shines so brightly still from the manger of Bethlehem. Cause this blessed influence not only to soften our hearts but to cleanse them of sin and selfishness and to strengthen them for the tasks and duties of this all-important hour. May Christ be born in many hearts that know Him not and be given full place in those hearts that have professed to know him yet have kept Him crowded into a corner. In His name we ask it. *Amen.*

CHRISTMAS

1

"The unsearchable riches of Christ."
—EPHESIANS 3:8.

MAY THE RICHES of Thy grace in Christ Jesus, O God, occupy a more important place in our lives than the riches of this present world. While we would not despise nor hold lightly any good thing, help us to put the better ahead of the good and to place the best on the topmost pinnacle of life. May there be no lowering of our highest Christian standards as we celebrate the birth of Jesus, but rather an exalting of them during the holiday season. In the name of the Christ child. *Amèn.*

CHRISTMAS

1

*"Lo, the star . . . went before them, till it came
and stood over where the young child was."*
—MATTHEW 2:9.

O LORD, let the unutterable sweetness of the life of Jesus breathe through the spirit of Thy people at this Christmas time. Cause the light that radiates from lives truly devoted to Thee to glow so brightly during the coming days that men who know Thee not will stop to wonder and begin to yearn for the hidden source of such spiritual beauty. And having turned to seek, may they find for themselves the manger of Bethlehem and, with it, life everlasting. In Jesus' name. *Amen.*

THE END OF THE YEAR

1

*"Thou art the same, and thy years shall not
fail."*—HEBREWS 1:12.

LORD, Thou hast been the dwelling
place of Thy people in all generations.
Thou art our sure defense today. As
the years come and go, may we continually abide in Thee with whom a
thousand years are but as one day. In
the timeless presence of God and forti-
fied with His grace, make us willing and
glad to serve, in the midst of time, our
day and generation, being assured that
service to men in Thy name is service to
Thee. And when our work here is
ended, put us to work anew in the land
where dwell the spirits of just men
made perfect. For Christ's sake. *Amen.*

PRAYERS

FOR SPECIAL OCCASIONS

OPENING OF SCHOOL

1

*"And Jesus increased in wisdom and stature,
and in favour with God and man."*
—LUKE 2:52.

FATHER IN HEAVEN, we bring to Thee for Thy blessing our children who are starting back to school again. Precious as they are to us, we know that they are more precious to Thee. Keep them during the coming days from physical harm. Watch over them as they cross the crowded streets. Guide them as they renew old friendships and seek new ones. May their hearts be kept pure, their lives clean, and their spirits fresh and bright. Help them to grow, day by day, as our Master grew when He was a lad at Nazareth, long, long ago—in wisdom and stature, and in favor with God and men. We pray in the name of Him who took little children in His arms and blessed them. *Amen.*

GRADUATION DAY

1

"Keep that which is committed to thy trust."
—I Timothy 6:20.

O MASTER, we thank Thee for the fresh young lives of our boys and girls, trained in our schools, and now ready to set forth into the world to find their places of service. Guide them, unerringly, with Thy hand into the work which Thou hast appointed them. Let none hold life lightly, nor carelessly spend the precious years allotted them. May all, grateful for their opportunities, mindful of their responsibilities, and eager for heroic and unselfish tasks in a distracted world, be used by the Lord of men and nations in carrying to completion His wise and loving plans. For Jesus' sake. *Amen.*

WEDDING DAY

"And both Jesus was called, and his disciples, to the marriage."—JOHN 2:2.

MASTER, we would call Thee to the marriage today, remembering that Thou didst respond to such a call in the long ago. Without Thy presence and without Thy blessing, there can be no true union of hearts and lives at the marriage altar. Help us to hold sacred the institution that Thou didst bless in such a wonderful way in Cana of Galilee. Deliver us from anything, without or within, that might mar the beauty, disturb the harmony, or shorten the length of this relationship that should be, and can be, the most satisfying and blessed of all life's experiences. Our voices are lifted to Thee in prayer for Thy grace in the deep experiences that marriage brings. In Thy name. *Amen.*

GRADUATES FROM
THEOLOGICAL SEMINARIES

"Sanctify them through thy truth: thy word is truth."—JOHN 17:17.

OUR MASTER, we pray Thee to bless in a very special way the young men who are graduating at this season from our theological seminaries. Let Thy divine care attend them as they go out into the world to become spiritual and religious leaders. May they be true ambassadors of God, faithful stewards of the mysteries of the gospel. Imbue them with the spirit of sacrificial service. Guide them unerringly to the places of service Thou hast appointed unto them, and give them rich ministries in the service of God and in service to their fellow men. Help them to keep that which is committed unto them and to prove faithful unto the trust, we ask in Thy name. *Amen.*

CHURCH COURTS

"Let each esteem other better than themselves."
—PHILIPPIANS 2:3.

O GOD, let Thy guiding presence be felt in all the sessions of church courts that convene at appointed times. May the members ever be mindful of the Head of the Church, zealous for His honor, and eager in His service. In their relationship with one another may the Spirit of Christ be manifested, correcting human faults and soothing disagreements and irritations whenever they arise. Be pleased to work through men, who are at best but imperfect human instruments, in the advancement of the cause of our Master. Overrule mistakes that may be made, and strengthen fearful hearts should any falter in the cause of right. In Jesus' name. *Amen.*

CHURCH COURTS

*"The wisdom that is from above is first pure,
then peaceable."*—JAMES 3:17.

VISIT WITH THY PRESENCE, our
Father, and direct by Thy Spirit, the
courts of the churches which are, and
will be, in session during this season of
the year. May the body of Christ on
earth give evidence continually that it
is in touch with its Head in heaven.
Let wisdom from the Head be found in
all branches of the church below. May
the gospel of love, which the church
proclaims to the world, be seen in active operation as its members work out
plans and purposes for the days ahead.
In everything cause the name of Jesus
to be glorified and His cause magnified,
we ask for His sake. *Amen.*

COMMUNION

1

"For as often as ye eat this bread, and drink this cup, ye do shew the Lord's death till he come."—I CORINTHIANS 11:26.

WE PRAISE and bless Thy name, O Lord, as we gather at Thy table in obedience to Thy command. We thank Thee for the fellowship that we find here with the saints and with Thee. May the precious elements that we receive bring joy and peace and strength to our hearts. Send us forth from this holy place purified and refreshed. May we take up our tasks in the church and in the world with an unconquerable faith because we have here been again assured of our Master's return without sin unto salvation. May this living hope sustain us through the days ahead even though Thy mercy should send us peril, toil, and woe. This we ask in His blessed name. *Amen.*

COMMUNION

1

"This do in remembrance of me."
    —LUKE 22:19.

OUR FATHER, refresh Thy people as they meet together to partake of the sacred elements of the Lord's Supper. Let those who cannot be present also have their souls refreshed as they commune with Thee and with their brethren in spirit and in truth. May life become a sacrament to us all, so that not only at stated periods, but every day, we may live sincerely, earnestly, and faithfully with Christ as our spiritual companion and host. In His name. *Amen.*

PRAYER BEFORE OFFERING

"Though he was rich."
—II CORINTHIANS 8:9.

CREATOR OF ALL THINGS, increase the grace of liberality within the hearts of all Thy children. Let the thought of the sacrifice of our Master, His giving of Himself for our redemption from sin, inspire us to generous giving to all causes of His church. Permit us not to escape from recognition of the fact that nothing less than a tenth of our material possessions given to the Lord's work is promised a blessing in the Holy Scriptures. Shame us with the knowledge that even much less than this would amply provide for all the projected work of the church and permit an advance such as we have never yet experienced. Forbid that we should be among those who frustrate the grace of God. For Jesus' sake. *Amen.*

PRAYER AFTER OFFERING

1

*"The earth is the Lord's, and the fulness
thereof."*—PSALM 24:1.

O GOD, since all created things are Thine by right of creation, we cannot give to Thee that which is already Thine own. May we experience joy as we have brought to Thy altar a due portion of the material wealth that Thou hast entrusted to us as stewards. Transform our offering from that which is material to spiritual power which shall go forth from this place to strengthen the cause of Christ in the uttermost parts of the earth. Thanks be unto God for His unspeakable gift— the gift of His Son, and the gift of the liberal, sacrificial spirit of His Son incarnated in so many humble, trusting servants of the Lord. In His name. *Amen.*

END OF THE CHURCH YEAR

*"The Lord hath done great things for us;
whereof we are glad."*—PSALM 126:3.

ALMIGHTY GOD, we thank Thee for the times when Thou hast blessed us beyond our expectations and hast been more gracious unto us than we have asked or even thought. May all such experiences permanently strengthen our faith, increase our courage, and rejoice our hearts. Let the goodness of God continually lead us to repentance. Thou hast been very good to us as a church and as a people during the past year. The measure of Thy favor has been far beyond that which we deserve. We thank God and take courage as we look out upon the new church year. Throughout the days ahead grant that we may ever press toward the mark for the prize of the high calling in Christ Jesus, our Saviour and Lord, in whose name we pray. *Amen.*

VACATION TIME

1

"Jesus . . . being wearied . . . sat thus on the well."—JOHN 4:6.

MASTER, refresh with rest, wholesome pleasure, and the joys of congenial fellowship all who set forth upon their vacation season. May none return exhausted because of the wrong use of that which might have been a blessing. May all who are thus privileged lay up physical and emotional reserves for the days ahead and return to their work eagerly, with new strength and courage. For Jesus' sake. *Amen.*

PRAYERS

FOR SPECIAL NEEDS

THE ARMOR OF GOD

1

*"There is no restraint to the Lord to save by
many or by few."*—I SAMUEL 14:6.

OUR FATHER, in the midst of the
complicated situations of life and the
unsolved problems of the world, deliver Thy servants from any sense of
futility and Thy church from any attitude of defeatism. Cause us to understand that God's power has never
been obstructed by difficulties nor His
love limited by the confusion of human
plans. May the very failure of man's
best resources impel us toward the resources of God and induce us, however
unwillingly, to make larger use of
spiritual powers and the unseen but ir-
resistible forces they contain. For Jesus'
sake. *Amen.*

ALIVE

1

"The gate of the temple which is called Beautiful."—ACTS 3:2.

KEEP US ALIVE, O Lord, to the beauties of the world, to the joys of friendship, and to the wonders of Thy grace each day that we live. May we spend all our years in the sunshine of Thy presence. Verify in our experience the wonderful promise of Scripture that the path of the righteous is as the dawning light which shineth more brightly unto the perfect day. Whatever our outward condition may be, or become, make our souls glow always with a celestial brightness and shape our lives so that they will be a blessing to our fellow men. For Jesus' sake. *Amen.*

FISHERS OF MEN

*"Come ye after me, and I will make you
to become fishers of men."*—MARK 1:17.

OUR FATHER, keep us ever re-
minded that our Master's purpose on
earth, according to His words, was to
seek and to save that which was lost.
As His followers, and as those who
have been saved by His gracious power,
may we make it the business of our lives
to lead others to Him that they, too,
may be saved. Let our hearts continue to trouble us so long as there are
those out of Christ whom a loving,
sympathetic, and urgent word from us
might turn to Him. Impress it upon
our souls that it is not Thy will that
one should perish, but that all should
come to repentance. Grant unto us not
only zeal in this great work, but also
winsome attractiveness and spiritual
power. In Jesus' name. *Amen.*

OUR NATION

1

"God be merciful unto us, and bless us."
—PSALM 67:1.

LORD OF EVERY LAND and nation,
we thank Thee for men whose faith in
Thee has made them great in the his-
tory of our country. Make us realize
that only those lands are truly pros-
perous and happy whose leaders are led
by the Spirit of God. As we give Thee
thanks for courageous Christian lead-
ership in the days gone by, we pray
Thee for men at the head of affairs in
our nation during these troubled days
in whose hearts is the fear of the Lord
and whose greatest ambition is to serve
Thee and do Thy will. So shall our
beloved land fulfill the mission Thou
hast appointed unto it, and God, even
our own God, shall continually bless
us. In Jesus' name. *Amen.*

COLLECTIVE SINS

1

*"Let justice roll down as waters, and right-
eousness as a mighty stream."*
—AMOS 5:24.*

O KING OF NATIONS, we pray that
we may be set free both from those fail-
ings of which we are conscious and
from the defects of disposition that
keep us from seeing other shortcomings
that hinder our Christian usefulness in
the Kingdom at large. Give us a consciousness of guilt, not only for personal sins but also for the great collec-
tive sins of mankind, from which we
cannot escape a share of responsibility.
Help us to believe in the saving power
of the gospel when applied through the
lives of redeemed men to the sins of so-
ciety. Let us never be complacent or at
ease so long as our fellow men are un-
justly oppressed. In His name. *Amen.*

*American Standard Version.

PEACE

1

"On earth peace, good will toward men."
—LUKE 2:14.

OUR HEAVENLY FATHER, let the peace of God, of which the angels sang on the hills of Bethlehem, flow into the hearts of men throughout the world to-day. O Thou Prince of Peace, overrule all councils of men and nations that plan war, either presently or ultimately. Turn into foolishness the mad competition in the building of "engines of war and commotion." Prosper and further earnest efforts looking toward the reduction of national armaments and lifting from the shoulders of men the crushing burdens that preparations for war have placed there. May we learn to live at peace with one another and with Thee in everyday life. In the name of Him who left His peace as a parting gift to believers. *Amen.*

PEACE

1

"Neither shall they learn war any more."
—ISAIAH 2:4.

PRINCE OF PEACE, sharpen the ears
of Thy people at this Christmas season, so that above the noise of war,
strife, and sin of every kind they may
hear the words of the angels as they
still say: "Peace on earth, good will to
men!" Make us believe in peace—its
supreme necessity, its eventual possi-
bility, its surpassing value both for the
hearts of men and the lives of nations.
O Thou Christ of Peace and Good
Will, speak to our hearts anew as we
celebrate Thy birth and make us realize and understand that all possessions
and advantages that destroy or post-
pone peace can only be as wormwood
and gall. In Jesus' name. *Amen.*

OUR SCHOOLS

1

"The fear of the Lord is the beginning of wisdom."—PSALM 111:10.

O LORD, we thank Thee for our schools and for the teachers and others whose conscientious work has made successful the school year just closing. May all who love, believe in, and work with youth unite in seeking the way by which high ideals of life may be placed more effectively before our boys and girls. Let us not be satisfied with the training of the mind alone, but have as the supreme goal of our efforts in education the development of strong, Christian characters. For Jesus' sake. *Amen.*

THE BIRTH OF A CHILD

1

*"Now when Jesus was born in Bethlehem of
Judæa."*—MATTHEW 2:1.

DEAR GOD, in our joy at the coming of a new life into the world, a new
brightness into our homes, and a new
love into our hearts our thoughts turn
back in adoration and praise to the little Babe in the manger at Bethlehem.
We thank Thee, humbly and gratefully, for these messengers of light who
come to us from heaven and pray that
the life of this little one who means so
much to us, as well as the lives of all
Thy little ones, may be precious in Thy
sight and sacred in the sight of men.
For Jesus' sake. *Amen.*

YOUTH

1

"Remember now thy Creator in the days of thy youth."—ECCLESIASTES 12:1.

OUR FATHER, we give Thee thanks for our boys and girls with their fresh outlook upon life and their wealth of potential resources. Bless them with Thine own presence as they graduate from our schools and colleges at this season of the year. Grant that they may remember their Creator in the days of their youth. Make them mindful of the meaning which Thou alone canst give life. Help them to dedicate themselves to noble service and to high ideals. Grant them the satisfaction of genuine success and the joy of real accomplishment in the years ahead, we ask in Jesus' name. *Amen.*

THE HOME

1

"Let them learn first to shew piety at home."
—I TIMOTHY 5:4.

OUR HEAVENLY FATHER, teach us
how to make our homes and our home
life so beautiful that when we speak of
heaven as being our home, there will
be a longing in our hearts for the final
abode of the soul. Help us, as we build
in the home and out, to use always ma-
terials of permanent and abiding quality, knowing that it is foolish to give
ourselves to those things which will
not last so long as we. May the pain
of every failure and the sting of every
disappointment be forgotten in the constant sense of Thy presence and the joy
of Thy companionship. For Jesus'
sake. *Amen.*

IN THE PRESENCE OF DEATH

1

"I am the resurrection, and the life."
—JOHN 11:25.

O GOD, it is only Jesus who can interpret to us our sorrows and help us to bear them bravely. We thank Thee that He who tasted death once for all men has told us that because He lives, we shall live also. In this confidence, may we look upon the passing from our eyes of the ones we love as being a transfer of citizenship from earth to heaven, of church membership from the church militant to the church triumphant. Rather than call them back, help us to make ourselves ready to join them when Thou dost summon us to a glad and unending reunion in our heavenly home. For Jesus' sake. *Amen.*

DECISIONS

"How long halt ye between two opinions?"
—I KINGS 18:21.

OUR MASTER, in the face of the many choices that life increasingly brings, help us to make right decisions and to walk in right directions. Keep us from indecision, lack of purpose, insincerity, and compromise, all of which unfit us for true Christian service and make life itself a burden. Help us to choose, this day, whom we will serve; and may the supreme choice of Christ cause other and lesser choices in the Christian life to be easier when they are faced and surer of being made aright. In His name. *Amen.*

MAKING DECISIONS

1

"Mary hath chosen that good part, which shall not be taken away from her."

—LUKE 10:42.

O WONDERFUL COUNSELOR, we pray that amidst the many things which influence us in making decisions, God's pure and loving Spirit may over-rule all that is unworthy. Help us to choose the "good part" and to be assured that that which is good shall not be taken away from us. Cleanse our hearts of selfishness, impurity, and guile. Grant that all questions immediately before us may be made so plain that we shall have no forebodings as we make our decision, nor vain regrets after it is made. For Jesus' sake. *Amen.*

MISSIONS

1

*"Go ye into all the world, and preach the
gospel to every creature."*—MARK 16:15.

O GOD OF ALL THE EARTH, may we
ever be mindful that we are, as Christians, followers of a missionary Saviour and children of a missionary God.
As God's yearning missionary heart
provided a way of salvation for us, so
may we, with missionary fervor, share
our blessings with our brethren wherever they may be—close at hand or far
away. Grant that the missionary zeal
of the early church may glow again in
the hearts of Christians, and that we
may count it our highest joy—as well
as our inescapable duty—to execute
the Lord's last command and carry the
gospel to all the ends of the earth. In
Jesus' name. *Amen.*

MISSIONS

1

"Let the peoples praise thee, O God."
—PSALM 67:3.*

LORD, we would praise Thee not only with our lips but also with our lives. Help us to keep constantly before our minds the words of Jesus: "Why call ye me, Lord, Lord, and do not the things which I say?" May we show forth Thy praise in Christlike lives, in loyal service both in and out of the church, and in faithfulness to the task of carrying the gospel to all lands so that the peoples of every nation may know Thy name and praise Thy grace. Keep us from being diverted from our great commission by an overzealousness that is divisive, or a complacency that is deadening, or a liberalism of conduct and belief that is deluding. For Jesus' sake. *Amen.*

*American Standard Version.

THE SINFUL

1

*"I came not to call the righteous, but sinners
to repentance."*—MARK 2:17.

O LORD, surely the gospel records
show us that Jesus never despaired of
the salvation of any sinful man who
longed to be freed from the bondage of
sin. May we never lose hope, nor cease
our efforts and prayers, on behalf of
those who have fallen by the wayside.
Let us never despair of those who still
wander in paths of iniquity. Call them
back from death with Thy loving voice
and woo them with Thy tender compassion. Use us in any way Thou
pleasest to snatch them as brands from
the burning. Make us willing, not only
to pray and labor, but also to suffer and
sacrifice until those we love and Thou
dost love are rescued from the Evil
One and are saved by grace, through
faith. In His name. *Amen.*

ON LEAVING HOME

1

*"Wist ye not that I must be about my
Father's business?"*—LUKE 2:49.

HELP US to realize, O Lord, that the
shelter of home and the protection of
loving parents cannot be ours always.
As we find that our life's mission calls
us away from those we love so dearly
and from homes that have become so
precious, we pray that we may feel the
touch of Thy hand on ours and ever
be led in the paths of righteousness for
Thy name's sake. Help us to find our
places in the world and to invest all our
God-given talents in work and service
that are honorable, profitable in the
very best sense, and needed by our fellow men. May we ever be true to ourselves, true to our friends and loved
ones, and supremely true to Thee who
art our Lord and Master. In Thy name
we pray. *Amen.*

THE TEMPTED

1

"Lead us not into temptation."
—MATTHEW 6:13.

OUR FATHER, we pray that God may lighten the temptations to evil of all those whose strength is small. Let them not yield even in their most secret thoughts, nor gratify with their minds the desires which they have thus far resisted in their outward behaviour. Teach them to think upon things that are true, honorable, just, pure, lovely, and of good report; and may the virtue and praise of these qualities of life be worked steadily and steadfastly into their characters. In the midst of every struggle, encourage them with the thought that each victory that is won makes other victories easier and more certain. For Jesus' sake. *Amen.*

PRAYERS

FOR LITTLE CHILDREN

MORNING PRAYER

I pray Thee, Lord, to keep me good
And kind and true, throughout this
    day.
Help me to do the things I should
With brave and cheerful heart, I pray.
For Jesus' sake. *Amen.*

✝

EVENING PRAYER

Lord, Thou hast kept me safe this day,
Now keep me through the night.
Cleanse me from every sin, I pray,
My soul make pure and bright.
For Jesus' sake. *Amen.*

MORNING PRAYER

Thy presence, Lord, throughout the
    night,
Hath kept me till the morning light.
Thy love protect me all this day,
And keep me pure and strong, I pray.
For Jesus' sake. *Amen.*

✦

EVENING PRAYER

Lord, as I kneel, this night, to pray,
My burdens at Thy feet I lay.
Refresh me through the night with
    sleep,
And all my loved ones safely keep.
For Jesus' sake. *Amen.*

GRACES

GRACE

Our Father, bless us as we eat,
Let love make every morsel sweet.
We thank Thee for Thy gifts this day.
May all our needs be met, we pray.
Amen.

✓

GRACE

Around this table, Lord, as we
Enjoy our food which comes from
    Thee,
May love with all things good be
    found,
And grateful thanks to Thee abound.
Amen.

✓

GRACE

Thank Thee, our Father, for our food
And all Thy gifts, for they are good.
Amen.

GRACE

Our Father, we thank Thee for Thy goodness in providing for the needs of our bodies and pray Thee that our daily bread may turn our hearts to God, who supplies both our physical and spiritual needs. *Amen.*

GRACE

Our Father, we thank Thee for this food that has been prepared, for those who have prepared it and, most of all, for Jesus Christ, who is the true bread of life. In His name. *Amen.*

GRACE

We thank Thee for Thy goodness,
　　Lord;
Bless Thou the family at this board.
Let love, from Thee, upon us shine,
And feed our souls with bread divine.
　　For Jesus' sake. *Amen.*

I N D E X

I N D E X

· 184 ·